WORLD WINDOWS

Animal Groups

HEINLE
CENGAGE Learning™

Y|S|G
A YBM COMPANY
Young & Son
Global, Inc.

What is your favorite animal?

Contents

mammal

bird

fish

amphibian

reptile

insect

Animal Groups

Cats and dogs belong to the same animal group.

There are different groups of animals. Animals in each group may look different, but they are alike in some ways. All animals can be grouped by their features.

monkey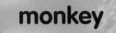

rabbit

fur

Mammals are animals that have fur or hair. They give birth to their young and feed them milk.

Monkeys and rabbits are mammals.

Birds

eagle

Birds are the only animals that have feathers. They have two legs and two wings. Most birds fly. They have their young by laying eggs.
Eagles and ostriches are birds.

ostrich

feathers

An ostrich cannot fly.

Fish

scales

angelfish

gill

tuna

Most fish are covered with scales and live in water. They have gills to breathe and use their fins to help them swim. Most fish also lay eggs. Angelfish and tuna are fish.

Amphibians

frog

salamander

Most amphibians
have smooth, wet skin.
They lay eggs in water. Most young
amphibians live in water, but they live on
land as adults. Some adult amphibians
can breathe both on land and in water.
Frogs and salamanders are amphibians.

Reptiles

snake

scales

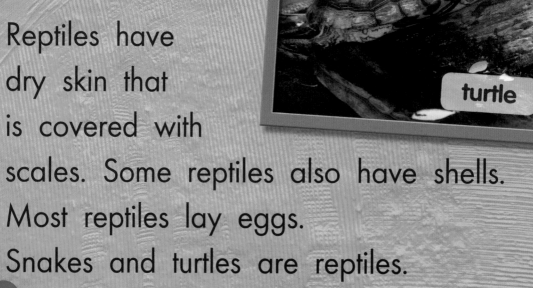

turtle

Reptiles have
dry skin that
is covered with
scales. Some reptiles also have shells.
Most reptiles lay eggs.
Snakes and turtles are reptiles.

12

Insects

Insects are animals that have three body parts and six legs. Most insects have wings and lay eggs. Many of them are very small compared to other groups of animals. Ants and bees are insects.

bee

ants

What are these animal groups?

Are Bats Birds?

Bats have wings and fly the way birds do. Does this mean they are birds? Bats have fur, not feathers. Bats do not lay eggs. They give birth to their young and feed them milk. So bats are actually mammals, not birds!

Glossary

amphibian
An animal that lives in water and on land

breathe
To take air into and out of the lungs

feature
An important part or aspect of something

feed
To give food to someone or something

give birth to
To produce live young

insect
An animal with three body parts and six legs

mammal
An animal with hair or fur that feeds milk to its young

reptile
An animal with dry skin that is covered with scales

Index